SISTERS
OF THE
HEART

SISTERS OF THE HEART

MIRIAM NEFF

Thomas Nelson, Inc.

Nashville • Atlanta • London • Vancouver

Published in Nashville, Tennessee, by Thomas Nelson, Inc., Publishers, and distributed in Canada by Word Communications, Ltd., Richmond, British Columbia, and in the United Kingdom by Word (UK), Ltd., Milton Keynes, England.

Library of Congress Cataloging-in-Publication Data

Neff, Miriam.
    Sisters of the heart / Miriam Neff.
        p.   cm.
    ISBN 0-7852-7744-7
    1. Women—Prayer-books and devotions—English.   2. Devotional
calendars.   I. Title.
BV4844.N45   1995
242'.643—dc20   95–24129
                                                                                    CIP

Printed in the United States of America

1 2 3 4 5 6 7 — 01 00 99 98 97 96 95

Dedicated to God and his Son, Jesus,
who are Lord of all
Because of them
we are sisters of the heart

Acknowledgments

*W*riting a book is aptly compared to giving birth: both are definitely worth the mild discomfort or agony. Neither is anything like the descriptions we've heard. Whether a baby of eternal magnitude or a book of temporary significance, neither is exactly like what we expected; both are shaped by the events during incubation.

This book is different from any I have ever written in that its incubation was the worst period of my life. I have a deeper understanding of injustice, a new awe that Paul was able to pen the Prison Epistles, and a new reverence for God, who promises to prove himself the winner of the battle though the evil one is apparently on an almost unstoppable roll.

I thank my support system at Maine West High School, the friends at coffee, and our lunch table who tenaciously refused to let me give up. Each woman has persistence greater than my own and compassion on which I have drawn: Dagny Gebert, Gay Jacobs, Jan McClellan, Mary Mueller, Mary Tabatt, Sandy Stubbings, Sharon Hayhurst, Sheila Warner, and Shirley Aberg.

Joyce Christensen, though not at our coffee table, supported me with more than her expertise in educational matters. She modeled masterful networking, whether in schoolroom or courtroom, whether eye to eye with a judge or with phone in hand.

Brigette and Steve Johnson, and Mary Whelchel and her band of encouragers all brought reality to God's promise that we are never alone. Paula Crespo, my neighbor, walked with me and listened.

And to Sue Ellen and Gary Griffin, through you as our sister and brother in Christ, this Scripture has new meaning: "And God is faithful; he will not let you be tempted beyond what you can bear. But when you are tempted, he will also provide a way out so that you can stand up under it" (1 Cor. 10:13 NIV). Doors opened because your hearts opened.

ACKNOWLEDGMENTS

I know that my faith will intersect with God's faithfulness at some future time. Today will be history and this current battle will be a distant memory. Because of all of you, I trust that this battleground will be fertile soil and a transforming harvest will rise in the sun.

ACKNOWLEDGMENTS

Introduction

*T*his little book is different.

You'll recognize some new sounds as you read Scripture verses. I do not always directly quote a translation or paraphrase. So where does this sound come from? Certainly I am not trying to write a new paraphrase. I am a counselor by profession, employed full time, a mother of four; I don't have time to retranslate. Simply, I'm a busy woman who loves God who has been reading my Bible as if my life depended on it.

Let me describe my Bible.

When I became a Christian, I was a graduate student at Northwestern University and an avid reader with a love for research. I would spread open my King James Bible, Strong's *Concordance, Vine's Dictionary,* and the *Treasury of Scriptural Knowledge* around me on my apartment floor.

When I read pronouns and nouns such as he, she, him, her, brother, and sister, I looked up those words in the original language to see if the verse was meant for me as a woman, for men only, or for both women and men. Twenty-five years ago I began using *woman* in the place of *man* and *she* in place of *he* whenever appropriate.

With regrets that I had never studied at a Christian institution, I asked God to be my teacher, my professor. I looked up each gender-related word to see if God meant instruction for me. Was I included in the lesson or promise, or was it for someone else? I knew nothing of what churches considered "politically correct" regarding roles. I simply loved God and wanted to know what instructions he intended me to follow.

The result of my work was a very personalized, blotchy Bible that I treasure as a middle-aged woman.

When I share these Scriptures with other women, I have discovered that we sense the direct call of God in our lives in a fresh and personal way. We experience a sense of sisterhood and recognize God's forthright, intimate summons to women standing together.

If your life, like mine, requires a deeper connection to

your Maker, I trust these musings from my moments with God will encourage you. I hope to stimulate thinking and questioning; God can stand intense, intimate scrutiny. In fact, he welcomes it.

You will hear the sounds of many familiar versions on these pages. My intention is to share my personalized way of interpreting sacred truths for this ordinary world.

My wish, from this sister's heart to yours, is that God speaks to you.

Sisters,
I do not consider myself yet to have taken hold of it.
But one thing I do, I forget what is behind.
I strain toward what is ahead
I press on to the goal.
There's a prize, and I've been called to win it.

Philippians 3:13 (NKJV with my paraphrase)

$\mathscr{D}$id you know that most Christian working women consider their jobs their calling? I recently surveyed twelve hundred Christian women, asking them to rank the rewards of their employment. The number one reward of work was *fulfilling my spiritual calling.*

Martin Luther King Jr. said, "If it falls to your lot to be a street sweeper, sweep streets like Michelangelo carved marble. Sweep streets as Shakespeare wrote pictures. Sweep streets so well that all the host of heaven will have to say, 'Here lives the street sweeper who did his job well.'"

The truth is women are working as though more than their lives depended on it. Women are working with passion beyond survival. Above the hum of computers, conveyor belts, telephones, vacuums, the white noise of offices, class-rooms, and hospital hallways, they press on because they hear God calling.

✐ **Our work is more than work; we're on the job for our God.**

Sisters, if being a Christian means anything real
  to you,
  if Jesus' love comforts you,
  if you have his Spirit,
Then be unified, not uniform.
Love each other and share the same goals.
Don't be motivated by selfish ambition or vanity.
Be humble, consider others more important than
  yourself.
Look out for your own interests (it's necessary).
Look out for the interests of others (it's higher
  living).

Philippians 2:1–4 (NKJV with my paraphrase)

$\mathcal{O}$n airplanes, in case of difficult flying conditions, parents are told first to secure their own oxygen mask, then they can secure their child's. Women are tempted to believe that the right choice is not to think of ourselves, but rather give ourselves totally to others. But when we give oxygen to another before we have secured our own supply, we flounder. We find ourselves depleted, used up, unable to go on. Having not loved ourselves, we are unable to love others.

Jesus showed us a higher standard for living when he went alone into the solitude of the hills around the Lake of Galilee. Retreating from those seeking his help, he spent time with his most favored person and intimate friend, his Father.

In our divided world, unity among sisters requires energy and persistence as never before. Unity of hearts will shrivel quickly without straight, clear-headed, practical unity. But we cannot give to each other what we do not possess ourselves.

✐ **Give yourself permission to take care of yourself.**

Finally, sisters, stay focused.
If it's true, noble, if it's right, pure, lovely, if it's
admirable, if it's excellent,
Keep it in center focus.
The God of peace will be with you.

Philippians 4:8–9 (NKJV with my paraphrase)

One Easter Sunday morning, Marian Anderson was scheduled to sing at Constitution Hall in Washington, D.C. The hall was owned by the Daughters of the American Revolution who refused to allow her to perform there—because she was black.

Eleanor Roosevelt heard of this. Eleanor could have said, "This is wrong; I hope someday she can sing anywhere." She could have said, "I can't change building use policies; I am powerless."

Thank God, Eleanor Roosevelt was a woman of courage who simply did what she could.

SISTERS OF THE HEART

Thank God, Marian Anderson stayed focused on singing though her heart must have felt seared.

Eleanor arranged for Miss Anderson to sing from the steps of the Lincoln Memorial. Seventy thousand people crowded around to hear her, and millions more heard her on radios. She became a symbol of liberation by breaking through the racial walls in musical organizations.

I believe that God was singing high above the capitol of our nation that Easter Sunday morning.

✍ **I believe women make a difference when we keep God center focus.**

Both the one who makes women holy and those who are made holy are of the same family. So Jesus is not ashamed to call them sisters. He says, "I will declare your name to my sisters; in the presence of the congregation I will sing your praises."

Hebrews 2:11–12 (NIV with female nouns)

$\mathcal{I}$ am sometimes surprised at the things women feel bad about. We carry guilt over the junk we did in our preteen years, our teen years, and every year thereafter.

How can this be? If Jesus tells us he sings our praises, how can we drag through life shouldering guilt? Our Father says he forgave every wrong thing we ever did the moment his Son died for us. It's history, sister. We are positioned as sisters to Jesus, God's daughters; both Jesus and his Father find us delightful. Jesus sings about us.

May I illustrate from my experience as a little farm girl? Life reminds me of opening the sagging wooden gate and stepping into our delightful southern Indiana meadow. I was free to run. Running barefooted through soft clover, I went from dry earth to the soggy grasses near the pond. Cow pies dotted the meadow. I was made to run; God wired me that way. But I stepped in a lot of stuff on the way to the pond.

And then God washed my feet. They are clean.

I have seen women's postures change when they learned their position as God's daughter. When we know we're forgiven, we stand tall. No wonder. Remember, we need carry no baggage.

🖎 **Sisters, God is never ashamed of us.**

Therefore, I urge you, sisters, since God has mercy, offer your body as a living sacrifice, holy, pleasing to God.

That's how you worship him.

Don't conform to this world.

Be transformed, deliciously different, with a new mind.

Then God's will is tested and proved in your life. And his will is good, pleasing, and perfect.

Romans 12:1–2 (NIV with my paraphrase)

*W*hat's so special about quilts? After all, aren't they just little pieces of fabric, some stitches, and backing?

You won't want to ask those questions of quilt lovers unless you have hours to listen. They will tell you the history of the scraps of fabric, of dresses worn by sisters and grand-mothers. Of smocks they remember on their aunts, of sun-dresses, tablecloths, and even drapes. They will describe to you the laying out of the design, the careful rearranging, the quilt frame dominating the living space, as well as time.

Though the scraps no longer cling to the perspiring shoulders of working women or provide protection for wooden tables, they are not sacrificed. They are living again. Transformed by a new design, to a new function. More precious now with a new function, quilts show us that deliciously different, in God's hands, is good.

✍ **Lord, may these changes in my life show the world, and me too, that you are good.**

For by God's grace I say to every woman,
  don't put yourself on a pedestal, or in the dirt.
Realistically see yourself with the faith God has
      given you.
Each of us (women and men) has a body of
      different parts.
The sisterhood has different parts
  and we are part of Jesus' body, the church.
We have different gifts that vary due to the grace of
      God.
If a woman's gift is prophecy, let her prophesy with
      faith.
If a woman's gift is serving, let her serve.
If a woman's gift is teaching, let her teach.
If a woman's gift is encouraging, let her
      encourage.
If a woman's gift is helping through giving,
  let her do it with generosity.
If a woman's gift is leadership,
  let her govern with diligence

If a woman's gift is showing mercy,
let her do it cheerfully.

Romans 12:3–8 (NIV with my paraphrase)

*H*ave you ever hidden a gift?

I once received a beetle watch. When you pinch its wings, they open to reveal the watch face. It's not really me. It has been in the back of a drawer—for years.

Appropriate? Yes, I needed a watch.

Just not that watch. It's not the right match.

God's gifts are different. They are appropriate because he first made us and then gave us a gift to match.

We hear many voices. "*You* can't do that."

And we slide the gift to the back of the drawer.

"Your gift is, well, small. We need bigger gifts here."

"Your gift is no good. We need fancy gifts here."

Nike ads say, "Just do it."

Our Creator, our gift giver, says do it with faith, courage, cheer, generosity, and diligence.

I think I'll dig out that beetle watch and wear it as a reminder. Different is okay.

✐ **God-given gifts are always usable, always good.**

MIRIAM NEFF

Do not be overawed when a woman grows rich,
  when the splendor of her house increases;
    for she will take nothing with her when she dies,
    her splendor will not descend with her.
Though while she lived she counted herself
      blessed—
    and women praise you when you prosper—
    she will join the generation of her mothers,
    who will never see the light of life.
A woman who has riches without understanding
  is like the beasts that perish.

Psalm 49:16–20 (NIV with female nouns)

*M*y grandmother died at age ninety-seven, leaving little but a sturdy suitcase packed with a few cotton dresses and talcum powder. These words were crowded efficiently onto three small sheets of paper:

18

SISTERS OF THE HEART

Some things I have done and helped to do.
All kinds of farm work, including plowing,
hoeing, ditching, grubbing, mowing, binding,
and cutting grain by hand; stacking
wheat, oats, and hay; threshing by hand with
a flail made from hickory bushes,
breaking and training young horses and mules,
feeding and taking care of farm animals,
blacksmithing and shoeing horses and mules;
clearing new ground and burning off same,
sawing down trees and helping split
them into rails, posts, boards, and
shingles; making spokes and ax handles,
hauling rails and building miles of
rail, and other kinds of fences
including stone fence; digging post holes, making gates,
bars, doors, sawing,
splitting, and hauling wood; making
barrels, wagons and wagon beds; building
dry kilns of stone, and drying pears,
apples, and peaches on same; laying
foundations, erecting and moving buildings;
painting, digging cellars, carpentering,
making maple sugar and syrup, also sorghum,
stripping, cutting, and hauling the
cane to the mill. Taking wool to the carder

MIRIAM NEFF

and spinning the rolls into yarn, weaving,
filling quills and shuttles, winding
and reeling the yarn into hanks and skeins;
cutting carpet rags and helping to warp
and put the carpet chain through
the sleys; braiding and knitting rugs,
stockings, socks, and mittens; crocheting,
embroidering, tailoring, knitting lace,
and doing all kinds of sewing
including millinery; mending shoes.
Taking wheat and corn to mill on horseback,
making soap and lye hominy, butchering,
rendering lard, curing and canning meat
and making sausage, smoking the meat
after curing, with hickory chips and corncobs.
Grafting and setting out trees, general
orchard work, making cider and vinegar,
apple and peach butter, jams, preserves
canning, making jellies, all kinds of
pickles, relishes, sauces; gathered wild
fruits, berries, ginseng, wintergreen, yellow root,
and herbs. Raising poultry; beekeeping, assistant P.M.
clerk in a department store, housework,
nursing the sick and washing and dressing the dead.
Hunted and trapped wild animals and game
birds. Gathered nuts, walnuts, hazelnuts,

15

butternuts, chestnuts, chinquapins,
hickory nuts, and beechnuts. Market gardened
and taken many ribbons and prizes
at "fairs" and "farmer's institutes"
on fresh and canned fruits and vegetables,
pickles, jams, butters, and relishes. Made
comforts, pieced and quilted quilts,
picked ducks and geese and made a featherbed
and eight pillows. I have cooked with hot coals
on the hearthstone with skillet and lid,
on woodstove, coal stove, gas and electricity.
Made and studied by the light of
tallow candles, oil lamps, and electric lights.
Rode on horses, mules, and steers; in sleds, wagons,
buggies, carts, sleighs, carriages, buses,
street cars, trackless trolleys, autos, areo
trolley cars and railroad trains (locals, freights,
and passenger) drawn by coal, oil, and
diesel engines; in rowboats, a ship
on Lake Michigan and an ocean liner
on the Atlantic.

While I am impressed with her list, I am more impressed
by the title she gave her list:

The More Abundant Life of Hatie

16

She left me no measurable heritage, but she gave me a priceless gift. She left a cherished model; her words tutor me from the grave. She understood that abundant living is not about collecting things.

✐ **Every sister's life list can be one of abundant living. It's her choice, my choice.**

Wisdom makes one wise woman more powerful than ten rulers in a city.

Ecclesiastes 7:19 (NKJV with my paraphrase)

$\mathcal{D}$ee Jepsen, one of our sisters in Washington, D.C., leading the campaign against pornography, tells of her first impression of Mother Teresa.

Dee was attending a reception in honor of this famed woman. Dignitaries from all over the world, including the president of the United States, crowded the room. Thousands of dollars worth of dark suits straightened and stood as a tiny figure entered the room. Something about the little woman in scuffed shoes and a cotton sweater commanded the attention of everyone in the room. Her eyes were piercing, her voice strong with conviction when she spoke.

What was the source of this woman's power?

Not wealth, not political position, not a powerful organization.

"This meek little woman, who has sought no position, who has no worldly goods, and who is uncomfortable in the limelight, has been raised by God to a pinnacle of recognition. I'm told that this recipient of the Nobel Prize, when asked what she does, often responds that she is good at cleaning toilets."[†]

She saw what many eyes refuse to see. She felt and let passion overwhelm her life. She knew that she must act—and she did. And now rulers seek out her wisdom.

✐ **Political power pales beside the passion of a person on a mission.**

[†]Dee Jepsen, *Women: Beyond Equal Rights* (Waco: Word Books, 1984), 176.

MIRIAM NEFF

> *There is not a righteous woman on earth who does what is right and never sins.*
>
> Romans 3:10 (NKJV with my paraphrase)

"I'm not ready to try."
"I wouldn't get it right."
"I might only go halfway: I won't even start."
"I'm not good enough yet."

Voices inside us know 1,001 reasons we should never begin or excuses to wait for a strategic moment to begin.

Waiting to be perfect is a sure way to never begin. Expecting perfection of ourselves, we become our own worst taskmasters.

Where do we find courage to take action?

Every artist begins a masterpiece staring at a blank white space. Manuscripts are first empty papers. A corporation starts as a bright idea. A mission post is first one person's dream.

🖋 **Remember, after God created us, he looked at us knowing full well we'd never be perfect, and he said, "Good!"**

If anyone turns a deaf ear to the law, even her prayers are detestable.

Proverbs 28:9 (NIV with female pronoun)

Following all the rules is not politically correct these days. Most of us do not consider signs or instructions as absolutes. We read the signs and then decide which ones apply.

"No strollers on escalator." (That means don't take your stroller on the escalator unless you know how to do it. I know how, therefore the rule does not apply to me.)

"No food or drink in store." (This does not apply to ice-cream cones, because ice-cream cones do not belong in purses either. They can't be saved for later; therefore they must be carried into the store.)

"Speed limit 55 mph." (This is for people who don't live in this area and therefore do not know how to drive well at 68 mph on this particular road.)

The habit of selective obedience does not transfer well to our relationship with God. When we decide his instruction in one area does not apply to us, we erect a prayer barrier. We block communication with the One whose instructions are always good for us, always in our best interests, always for our welfare.

An unanswered prayer may be a signal to look for ignored instructions and to conduct a personal checkup for selective obedience.

✐ **Lord, have I given your Word a twist, so my attitude will fit my revised version? Have I pushed "fade" on a rule I don't like? Lord, restore my heart and my hearing.**

*The good woman brings good things out of the good
stored up in her heart, and the evil woman brings
evil things out of the evil stored up in her heart. For
out of the overflow of her heart her mouth speaks.*

Luke 6:45 (NIV with female nouns)

*D*oes your work sometimes stack evil in your mind
that trickles into your heart and fills you with anger and
bitterness? Some days are that way in my work.

Yesterday I felt polluted. One of my students was raped.
As her counselor, I listened, made phone calls, sat beside
her as she revealed her pain. Having suffered once, she
suffered again through the revelation to her mother, through
the questioning of the police. The process, while as tender
as we could craft it, could not but shake and pollute each
of us. Descriptions of gang tattoos, threats fulfilled, and evil
filled the room.

I have no defense able to stop the flow of evil in the

public high school where I work. But I hungrily gather the words of my Creator to stock my heart for each new day. My polluted environment need not pollute my heart.

Words of justice, words of compassion will never flow from evil hearts. But, sisters, God never turns his back on a hungry heart. He delights in throwing out pollution and filling us with goodness. And, heaven knows, this world needs good words from good women.

📎 **Lord, keep me hungry for you, nourished by your goodness.**

"But I tell you that women will have to give account on the day of judgment for every careless word they have spoken. For by your words you will be acquitted, and by your words you will be condemned." Matthew 12:36–37 (NIV with female noun)

That if you confess with your mouth, "Jesus is Lord," and believe in your heart that God raised him from the dead, you will be saved. For it is with your heart that you believe and are justified, and it is with your mouth that you confess and are saved. As the Scripture says, "Anyone who trusts in him will never be put to shame." Romans 10:9–11 (NIV)

"*G*ive me a break. I didn't mean it!" How often I have said all the wrong things at precisely the most destructive time. God could collect a mountain of my own words and stack them against me on judgment day. How the evil one likes to remind me of those words, especially the words I've said to my children.

But I have also confessed that Jesus is my Lord. And because of *those* words, I have been acquitted—pardoned, cleared, exempted from judgment, forgiven, reprieved.

Like my computer delete button that clears errors, confession clears careless words.

I remember a mountain of mistakes made by this over-eager mother raising my eldest child. Too many words, not the right words, jumbled words. A young adult now, living elsewhere, this daughter made a special phone call: "You told me I could do anything I set out to do. You believed in me, Mom."

Thank you, Lord, for hitting the delete button in her precious mind.

✏ **Good-bye shame and condemnation. Hello forgiveness and gratitude.**

A woman of many friends (meaning neighbor or acquaintance) comes to ruin, but there is a friend (meaning one who loves and shares goals) who sticks closer than a sister.

Proverbs 18:24 (NIV with my paraphrase)

"Hi! How are you?" your friend says passing in the hall.

You are halfway through answering and she is halfway out of earshot. You get the message. She didn't really care about your answer. Didn't care enough to slow down, anyway. Perhaps she's a neighbor, connected accidentally through geography or job. The Hebrew word for the first "friend" in the verse above has that meaning.

"What do you need from me this week to help you achieve your goals?" Your friend takes out her notepad and looks at you intently. Now this woman is F-R-I-E-N-D. She sticks closer than a sister. She is committed to helping you

SISTERS OF THE HEART

achieve your goals. This is the meaning of the second Hebrew word "friend."

Which friend am I? At times, shamefully, I consider how friends might be my personal assistants on the way to personal power and accomplishment. Then I am a user, not a friend.

"What do you need from me?"

"How can I help you?"

"What are you dreading ahead?"

"What would affirm you today?"

These are the sounds of sisters.

𝒟 **Today let me be a friend who sticks close and shares goals.**

Do not be deceived: God cannot be teased. A woman reaps what she sows. The one who sows to please her sinful nature, from that nature will reap destruction; the one who sows to please the Spirit, from the Spirit will reap eternal life.

Galatians 6:7–8 (NIV with my paraphrase)

$\mathcal{I}$ am forever refreshed by how direct God is. Real, genuine, no filler or blend, no coating or plating.

God is not into cover-ups, imitations, or look-alikes. Maybe that's why sometimes I just don't get it—who God is. He's so real, so direct. That's why you and I can ask tough questions, the ones hiding behind obvious answers and hard days. Do you ever wonder whether your life will make a difference? What good is life? What will be the result of any one of us having existed? What will be the harvest?

Lots of seeds look alike. You can mix lettuce, radish,

carrot, tomato, and zinnia seeds in your hand. They look similar. Toss them in the ground, see what they produce. Harvest time is revelation time.

Do you sometimes feel you fail? Are you feeling mother guilt? We parent the best we know how. We blunder and make mistakes, sure our children will remember the worst we have done. False guilt magnifies our mistakes. Most of us have not parented as well as we think we should. We have not pleased ourselves. Remember the harvest message: Progress from tiny seed to quality produce varies from type to type. Let's leave the final harvest with One who can't be deceived.

✑ **Have you put in your best effort on a task and the results appear futile and flimsy? Leave both the harvest and its timing in God's hands.**

Dear women, let us not love with words or tongue but with actions and in truth.

1 John 3:18 (NIV with female noun)

Now that you have purified yourselves by obeying the truth so that you have sincere love for your sisters, love one another deeply, from the heart.

1 Peter 1:22 (NIV with female noun)

Septima Clark was a foremother of the 1960s activists. Her father was a slave. She taught school in South Carolina. Joining the NAACP in 1919, she became involved in the struggle to equalize the pay of black and white teachers. Eventually she was discharged from teaching for her civil rights work.

Did she lose her voice when she lost her job? Hardly.

She embarked on a new career: teaching activists about community education and organization.

I take courage from Septima Clark. As with the truth about slavery, it's hard to find a place in some evangelical Christian circles where you can speak the truth about equality for women and priesthood of all believers. As with those speaking the truth about slavery, our voice cannot be silenced.

Septima Clark, ever the teacher though relieved of her teaching post, taught training classes for the NAACP. One of her students was Rosa Parks. Parks listened well. She attracted national interest in the massive civil rights movement when she refused to give up her seat to a white man on a Montgomery, Alabama, bus. Parks, a seamstress and secretary of the local chapter of the NAACP, was arrested for violating segregation laws.

I still remember the impact on me, a grade school girl in southern Indiana, of the newspaper photograph of a policeman fingerprinting Rosa Parks when she was arrested for not giving up her seat. Her back was erect. There was a look of calm on her spectacled face. Her full beautiful lips were closed, but I heard her voice.

While the names like Rosa Parks and Septima Clark may seldom be heard, their actions still speak. Devotion made them willing, and the rest is history.

Let us take courage from our sisters' actions. Love always hopes; love always perseveres.

🖊 **Young women, our daughters, following in our footsteps, are watching.**

But those who hope in the LORD will renew their strength. They will soar on wings like eagles; they will run and not grow weary, they will walk and not be faint. Isaiah 40:31 (NIV)

$\mathcal{I}$ don't know anything about soaring with eagles, but I know a bit about running.

Running my three miles one morning during another Chicago heat wave, the little hills in my town of Kildeer felt like mountains. Of course, my huffing and puffing might have been partly caused by the end of the school year, my emotional investment in a new radio program, and a few other things packed into my life. (I refuse to think that age affects my running ability!)

God sees me as a runner who need not grow weary. He sees me with incredible potential. He sees you and me as women who need not huff and puff through life.

He sees me running life's races and he knows I need

encouragement. I'm glad he told me that I could run and not grow weary. I'm glad he's given me examples of women who are running life's races with the aid of higher power.

My friend, Lynne, was running in a 15K Chicago marathon. She had trained halfheartedly for this race. After the 10K mark, she wished she'd trained more. She, like me, parented four children, and we were both full-time employees of a relocation company in Oakbrook. Lynne was becoming weary. She seriously considering calling it quits and forgetting her goal to finish.

She tuned in to a sound that had been in her ears since the beginning of the race, but had not heretofore caught her attention. It was the sound of noisy, rustling long pants. Running ahead of her was an older woman wearing long polyester pants that rustled like taffeta as she ran. This woman appeared to be nearing sixty years of age, and she was not correctly attired for running.

But she was ahead of Lynne.

Instead of dropping out at the next water table, Lynne grabbed a paper cup and, pouring water over her head, she refocused on her goal.

"If she can do it, I can do it."

And they both did.

✍ **Any woman can be a finisher. Any woman can soar.**

MIRIAM NEFF

So then, each of us will give an account of herself to God. Romans 14:12 (NIV with female pronoun)

$\mathcal{T}$he king of England wanted a different wife. He also wanted the blessing of the Catholic church. He could not have both, given the existence of his present wife and the policy of the church at the time. So he founded a new church: the Church of England. He selected leaders who would approve his desire for a different wife, his new policy for divorce, and probably any other idea he had.

Hence, he had a new church and, eventually, four other wives as well.

He could have saved himself years of incredible manipulation, the extermination of the few good men who challenged his ideas, and the termination of wives who did not please him if he had wanted God's blessing rather than men's. Even with the blessing of the new church he founded, he died a confused, dissatisfied dictator.

No human need found a church. God already did it, and he did it right the first time using Jesus as the cornerstone.

Besides founding his church, God keeps his own book of accounts. He does not reassign, delegate, or transfer the task to others. In the end, the king of England must answer neither to the church he abandoned nor to the one he created, but to God.

This is a good reminder to us today.

✍ **Women of integrity know whom they wish to please.**

May those who hope in you not be disgraced because of me, O Lord, the LORD Almighty; may those who seek you not be put to shame because of me, O God of Israel.   Psalm 69:6 (NIV)

$\mathscr{I}$ have often thought this verse admonished me to watch my tongue—I am prone to speaking quickly and thinking later. But in my world, I see that rather than impulsive, heartfelt words, the bigger problem is the silence of Christians. The apostles could not help but speak about what they believed, regardless of how their message was received.

I fear I have been silent too long about the position of children. We have allowed our world to prioritize personal pleasure, greed, and what works for bureaucracy and business above what is good for our kids.

May our children be spared the deafening silence of being devalued, ignored, or abandoned. May tired young mothers avoid the surrounding silent roar of poverty as they travel the maze that leads to no good life.

Who could speak better on behalf of needy children and impoverished women than Christian sisters who know the Author of Life? Who should speak if not Christian sisters whose passion rides on hope in One who fed five thousand with two fish and five loaves?

*✏ **Lord, help me discover a tiny platform from which to whisper for our children today. And tomorrow I shall ask for courage for the new day.***

But you are chosen women, a royal priesthood, a holy nation, a people belonging to God, that you may declare the praises of him who called you out of darkness into his wonderful light.

1 Peter 2:9 (NIV with female noun)

$\mathcal{T}$oday's woman cannot be defined. Tomorrow's woman, the woman of the twenty-first century will be even more diverse. While some might describe her as harried, trying to balance conflicting roles, she is in fact invigorated by the challenge. The Christian woman finds vitality and stimulation instead of pressure and stress. She is a living paradox of peace stepping into unknown positions in her work, her family life, and her faith. She thrives on challenge.

This two-thousand-year-old definition is the best: She is chosen—and she knows her position.

She is one of a royal priesthood—with constant, direct

48

communication with her Maker. There is never an indirect path or downtime when she cannot connect.

She belongs—she's part of a community beyond geography, beyond race, beyond special interests. Her community has no walls.

And she has a purpose—to be her Maker's advertisement and bring him applause.

🖋 **Stand tall, special woman. Remember your position.**

"Not by might nor by power, but by my Spirit,"
says the LORD Almighty. . . . "Who despises the
day of small things?"   Zechariah 4:6, 10 (NIV)

*R*obert Shurtleff enlisted in the Continental Army in 1781. He served nearly three years and was wounded twice. Then a doctor made a discovery. Robert Shurtleff was not a man, but a woman named Deborah Sampson. Her desire to help preserve her country was so great that she disguised herself as a man in order to serve. An indentured servant from Massachusetts, she felt compelled to fight for her country.

Did she have the spirit of Deborah the prophetess, the strength of Samson? She must have had some of both. Her husband received a military pension when she died.

She reminds us that valor is a virtue wherever exposed. And that inspiration often comes from small people. As an indentured servant, she knew that freedom was precious. Given liberty from her owner, she fought for a cause.

We are indentured, branded by the Holy Spirit of the Almighty, which becomes freedom indeed. Though we think ourselves small or powerless, the Spirit that empowers us is not restricted by our puny view of ourselves, our race, our status, or our gender.

Since the Lord Almighty has supplied us with his Spirit, we are women of substance; we have the right stuff.

🖋 **Lord, may who I am be magnified by your Spirit.**

*I assure you that there were many widows in Israel
in Elijah's time, when the sky was shut for three
and a half years and there was a severe famine
throughout the land. Yet Elijah was not sent to any
of them, but to a widow in Zarephath in the region
of Sidon. And there were many in Israel with
leprosy in the time of Elisha the prophet, yet not one
of them was cleansed—only Naaman the Syrian.*

Luke 4:25–27 (NIV)

$\mathscr{A}$re you ever distracted by asking "Why?"

Why does luck smile on her? Why does the door to the storehouse of blessing blow open just as she goes by carrying a shopping bag? Each woman has her own idea of what a storehouse of blessing is. For one, it's a healthy husband after age sixty. For another it's a husband, period. A kid with straight teeth. An impressive profession. Brilliant offspring. No Christian is immune from the temptation to ask, "Why her, not me?"

It's okay. God is neither shocked nor insulted. Asking "Why?" or any question can be a welcome beginning for talking to God. While he does not promise immediate answers, he promises immediate peace. Hunger goes on, sometimes illness or pain go on. Our child remains on the run or our crisis is just the beginning of a puzzling obstacle.

We need never feel bad about beginning any dialogue with God. He cannot be shocked or surprised. The lessons of Elijah and Elisha are that there are no insiders and outsiders, and God is deaf to no one.

✐ **Lord, after "Why?" let's talk about *how* I can live today.**

But now, this is what the LORD says—
  he who created you, O _____,
    [your name goes here]
  he who formed you, O _____:
"Fear not, for I have redeemed you;
  I have called you by name; you are mine."

"Bring my sons from afar
  and my daughters from the ends of the earth—
everyone who is called by my name,
  whom I created for my glory,
  whom I formed and made."

Isaiah 43:1, 6–7 (NIV with my paraphrase)

For you created my inmost being; you knit me
    together in my mother's womb.
I praise you because I am fearfully and wonderfully
    made;
  your works are wonderful, I know that full well.
My frame was not hidden from you when I was
    made in the secret place.

49

*When I was woven together in the depths of the
earth, your eyes saw my unformed body,
All the days ordained for me were written in your
book before one of them came to be.*

Psalm 139:13–16 (NIV)

*A*s I read Scripture about the source of life, I con-
clude that there is no such thing as an illegitimate person.
One neighbor used that term to describe my new adopted
son: "How can you love him as much as you love your
daughter, your own flesh?" His older sister, who was born
to me, raced ahead of us on her Little Tyke bike.

While I knew I must give her space to question and
wished to respond graciously, I wanted to run over her with
my baby buggy—even at the risk of awakening my new,
dearly loved son! Given my view of God, "illegitimate person" is an oxymoron.

If there's life, God is somewhere in the equation or he
will be. We may not see how or why at any given moment.
"Everyone . . . whom I made" means *every* one.

✐ **Lord, help me treat every person as your creation,
including myself.**

But whatever was to my profit I now consider loss for the sake of Christ. What is more, I consider everything a loss compared to the surpassing greatness of knowing Christ Jesus my Lord, for whose sake I have lost all things. I consider them rubbish, that I may gain Christ and be found in him, not having a righteousness of my own that comes from the law, but that which is through faith in Christ.   Philippians 3:7–9 (NIV)

*M*y name is Miriam. The days of my life were ordained according to Psalm 139. I am a farmer's daughter, the great-granddaughter of a tall, Cherokee woman with high cheekbones and dark eyes that flash with courage even through an aged tintype. Through good fortune, I was born in a time and place where girls were included in schooling. I have a bachelor's and master's degree from Northwestern University and a Phi Beta Kappa key, sixty-four graduate hours past a master's degree, and an administrative certificate.

I work in a public high school. I have a regular income from a good job that both challenges and brings me pleasure. Special projects include working with underachievers, Hispanic girls, and teen mothers. I have four children, two born to me and two adopted. I write. I have been married for twenty-nine years to a good man and I wish for no other.

What God has called me to do puts at risk the position my credentials earned me. I am called to remind the educational institution where I work that Christians are entitled to freedom of speech guaranteed in the Constitution. His calling requires me to be a voice reminding Christians that God created women with the same value as men and likewise gifted them. I have been surprised by those who wish me to be silent and surprised by encouragement when I least expected affirmation.

I do not understand. But I am not called to understand. I am called to be willing to give up anything and everything, called to obedience. Prophets in the Old Testament did not always know their enemy or understand why some people stood against them or for them. I guess I'm in good company.

✐ **Sisters, our definitions of profit and loss are different from the world's.**

MIRIAM NEFF

> *A wise woman has great power, and a woman of knowledge increases strength; for waging war you need guidance, and for victory many advisers.*
>
> Proverbs 24:5–6 (NIV with female noun)

The legacy of the Lone Ranger was a cloud of dust and the strains of the *William Tell Overture* ringing in our ears. He arrived on the scene at the right moment, rescued the damsel in distress, and disappeared.

Most of our problems today are not solved by a one-time intervention from a stranger. Looking at the big picture of real life, this rarely happens.

We need input from people who see from different vantage points. We need to collect wisdom from the smartest people we know. Women who listen to others are like a three-strand cord—stronger than the sum of their individual parts.

We can choose to make decisions alone. We can attempt

to solve problems like the Lone Ranger. But there's a better way. Your sister's path has been a bit different. She's collected different bits of wisdom. Her experience has not been exactly like yours. That's why you'll be a richer woman by gathering some of her advice, listening to her guidance. That's what sisters are for.

🖋 **Women around us are seldom there by coincidence. Tap into their experience, their wisdom.**

Put your trust in the light while you have it, so that you may become daughters of light.

John 12:36 (NIV with female noun)

*S*ow an act, reap a habit. Sow a habit, reap a character. This ancient saying describes how we become who we are. It applies to health, hygiene, vocabulary, etiquette, even exercise and the food we eat.

How do we become daughters of light? By following the pattern: act . . . habit . . . character. By performing one act at a time as women who see opportunity to build on the light we have.

When we have an opportunity to do good, we do it. When we can say a word that reflects our inner light from our Creator, we say it. We trust that God knows what knowledge we have and do not have, what opportunities we have and don't have.

He asks us to trust what we have, not what we wish

SISTERS OF THE HEART

we had. David, the shepherd boy, was proficient with a slingshot and used it. While preparing to fight Goliath, he was offered King Saul's armor including the big man's sword. He said, "No, thank you. I'm not used to those."

But he stepped onto the field trusting the small weapon he had. Years later, he confidently used the giant's oversized sword. "There's none like it. Give it to me."

Act with what you have: a little knowledge, a beginner's skill, a seed of compassion. More will come. Future possibilities, daughter of light, may bear little resemblance to today's opportunities. Take action.

🖋 **Trust what you have in hand today.**

Be still, and know that I am God.

Psalm 46:10 (NKJV)

$\mathcal{D}$o you feel God is absent, distant, unreachable, his line is busy? Often I recognize that I'm operating by remote control spiritually, and my world has become anything but "still."

What's a busy woman to do?

Pray for inner concentration. Pray that the reality that is God will penetrate our world again.

We may need to make room in our world for physical and mental stillness. Slow down. Lie down. Face the heavens. Breathing deeply of the air God provides, we can repeat our Creator's words to him and to our own hearts:

"Be still, and know that I am God."

Mental stillness seldom comes automatically to women today. Our lives are so complex: work, relationships, family; taking care of the roof over our head, the vehicle, the dripping faucet. We must create an environment for mental stillness.

Some of life's "stuff" must be put on hold; it should not be muddled over for a designated period of time. Some will wait, and some "stuff" is someone else's concern that, from time to time, we borrow.

Imagine placing what's on your mind on a shelf for a moment. In that time of mental stillness:

"Be still, and know that I am God."

✍ **Lord, quiet my soul in the midst of my world's clattering confusion.**

Therefore, my sisters and brothers, you whom I love and long for, my joy and crown, that is how you should stand firm in the Lord, dear friends!

Philippians 4:1 (NIV with my paraphrase)

*S*tand firm in the Lord? On my job? Some days this seems like an incredible, impossible assignment. I mean, to be blunt, just who does God think I am that I can stand firm where I work?

At times I think to be a counselor in a public high school was a bland career choice. This week I listened as students described witnessing attempted homicide—in their home. Police cars are regularly at the front entrance of the school. I work hard with pregnant girls. They have careened into two walls: one of seeing the world as too terrible to bring their child into, the second of believing the school environment too tough for them to stick it out and get that diploma.

Helping them over the second wall is my job, the first wall, my calling.

Has your work rocked you? Is it hard to be a woman of integrity: fair, honest, enthusiastic about getting the job done? Stand firm, Lord? How in this world?

The answer is in the "therefore." This not-so-spiritual-sounding word is there for a significant reason. It says, "Based on what I just said, the following is true."

In the previous paragraph, God tells me that I am a citizen of heaven. And I am here waiting for Jesus. He's coming. And he is going to transform my lowly body. (Which indeed on many days feels quite lowly.)

Therefore . . .

Just who does he think I am? A citizen of a higher country. A woman with future-oriented expectations. Standing firm because of who I am, regardless of what's coming down around me.

🖋 **Today is just the right day to stand firm.**

MIRIAM NEFF

So do not throw away your confidence; it will be richly rewarded. You need to persevere so that when you have done the will of God, you will receive what he has promised. For in just a very little while,

> *"He who is coming will come and will not*
> *delay.*
> *But my righteous one will live by faith.*
> *And if she shrinks back, I will not be pleased*
> *with her."*

Hebrews 10:35–38 (NIV with female pronouns)

*D*oes God's "little while" ever seem like an eternity to you? I wait for him to come into a situation and bring healing and resolution. And I wait, and I wait, and I wait.

How can we persevere when we don't know what to

do? I can take on another day of challenge with gusto if I have lots of things to do, when I know effective steps to take. Whether it's dirty laundry, cooking for a crowd, or taking care of four preschoolers, just let me at it. We can rise to challenges, can't we?

☆ Getting busy when I know the steps to a guaranteed outcome doesn't require faith. Faith is that tenacity to put one foot before another when you cannot see the earth your foot will rest on, when there is simply no good Plan A. A dry or ruined marriage, providing when employment is bleak, outwaiting and outloving a hate-filled teen—these are challenges with no simple Plan A. That's when God sees our perseverance as faith.

It was said during the Civil War, "These are the days that try men's souls." Men and women of courage fought tenaciously because they had a goal in their soul.

Sisters, we have a goal.

God will reward us for God-confidence with something beyond the immediate resolution to today's problems. We cannot even imagine what the reward will be.

We should not be surprised that we have days—and sometimes weeks, months, or bleak years—that try our souls.

Hurrying through O'Hare Airport, I step on a path with an automated voice that repeats, "Keep walking." That

62

message, though ever so ordinary sounding, offers spiritual advice.

"Keep walking, Sister," God whispers.

🖋 "I will bring resolution. I see your tenacity. But most precious to me, Daughter, I see your faith."

Sisters, if someone is caught in a sin, you who are spiritual should restore her gently. But watch yourself, or you also may be tempted. Carry each other's burdens, and in this way you will fulfill the law of Christ. If anyone thinks she is something when she is nothing, she deceives herself. Each one should test her own actions. Then she can take pride in herself, without comparing herself to somebody else, for each one should carry her own load.

Galatians 6:1–5 (NIV with female pronouns)

"Carry each other's burdens."

"Each one should carry her own load."

Sounds like a contradiction, doesn't it?

God is talking about two different kinds of problems. Burden means heavy sins so large they are team-sized. Load means something like a soldier's backpack, a pack that can't be split between two people. Nobody can help you.

SISTERS OF THE HEART

Have you ever admired a restored home filled with beautiful antique furniture? Its elegance is rich with character that comes only with time and real living. Sisters have that potential to be like furniture with the patina of life. Bonds of character forged of forgiveness and shared burdens create our community, our home. Leaders marked with vulnerability and humility are the foundation. Sisters restored.

Sisters helping to restore sisters. I believe this may be a lost art in the body of believers today. We do not do such a good job of calling each other to accountability. We may *know* each other's sin. We may discuss, advise, and criticize. But restore? How? This account tells of two methods.

Team-sized sins require a community of caring people to expose, confront, and help. Alcoholics Anonymous calls it intervention. People who care confront the person who is destroying herself and others. You don't have to be perfect, but you have to be strong.

We all have those "load-sized," very private problems, individual sins that can only be shouldered alone. We alone account to God for what we have done violating his way. Shouldering our own backpacks, we get on our knees and agree with God that he was right. Then, it's God-approved to have a sense of pride—inner satisfaction from having done the right thing. What are the temptations of the strong Christian sister confronting another? She may believe she is above slipping herself. She may believe her strength is self-secured. Both myths make her vulnerable.

Beautifully restored homes look out of sync filled with shabby furnishings. Fine antique furniture looks misplaced in a decrepit home. In the same way, neither method of restoration from sin can ever exist alone.

When we see another trapped sister and team together to confront sin, we cannot help but sense God's searchlight on our own behavior and motivation. If we don't bow and confess our private sins, we have no power to confront.

May this be a great decade of restoration.

✐ **Lord, show me which burdens are individual size and which are team size. Give me courage to shoulder some and share the rest.**

I care very little if I am judged by you or by any human court; indeed, I do not even judge myself. My conscience is clear, but that does not make me innocent. It is the Lord who judges me.

1 Corinthians 4:3–4 (NIV)

*W*ho do you pick to assess you? Some women have adopted their mom's view of themselves; other women have listened more to their dad's assessment of who they are. My sister, Linda, describes the assessors in her mind as a whole board of directors: Papa, Mama, her ex-husband. She even gave each of her three children a padded leather chair at the board table! Everybody told her who she was.

Linda is a recovering alcoholic now and quite proudly announced that she fired the board. She has learned that you can love a person without giving them power to define who you are.

Having a board of directors makes self-assessment easy.

They make the good/bad choices for you. Their yardsticks do the measuring. Criteria based on outcome is selected; they judge by what they can see or measure. Comparison charts are invented, and we weigh in, sometimes literally.

But no one else knows the inner obstacles to our obedience or what God is calling *us* to do or be. They can offer feedback on our behavior based on Scripture; they cannot evaluate our obedience.

Who sits on your board of directors? Who defines your success or failure? Who tells you who you are? Consider that the One who made you, who gave you life and the air you breathe, has already earned the position. He does no hostile takeovers. He comes only by your invitation.

✐ **Lord, be my loving board of directors.**

If one falls down, her friend can help her up.
But pity the woman who falls and has no one to
help her up!

Ecclesiastes 4:10 (NIV with female pronouns)

$\mathcal{M}$ay I encourage you to start a file of women who encourage you and teach you? You can find their stories in newspapers, magazines, books, and newsletters. I have been taught lessons of accountability by women who don't know me—but their example is real.

My file includes women who weren't perfect role models. We can learn from their successes—and their mistakes. One such woman was Aimee Semple McPherson. She preached, pastored a church, started a denomination, and initiated the first Christian radio station. However, like Saul, Israel's first king, she took a tumble.

Aimee Semple McPherson, a preacher so successful she eventually established her own church, seemed preordained for the ministry. Her mother brought her into the Salvation Army where she was a celebrated public speaker at age thirteen. By age thirty, the evangelist was quite possibly the most famous woman in America. Her first husband died in China, and she left her second husband, Harold McPherson, behind in Rhode Island. Her preaching stunned a crowd of fifteen thousand in London's Albert Hall, and she established the Foursquare Gospel Church International.

The story of her tumble from her calling reminds me of David's experience with Bathsheba. Nathan the prophet confronted David with his sin. But, sadly, Aimee Semple McPherson did not have a sister in her life to call her to accountability.

She became involved with a handsome radio engineer, Kenneth Gladstone Ormiston. Ironically, one of her accomplishments, being the first owner of a radio station owned by a religious organization (her church), played into a sad chapter of her life. She disappeared with this man for thirty-two days. When she reappeared, she told a ridiculous story that many people did not believe. National media reported her story with derision and laughter. Many of her followers still adored her, but from a distance. They adored her charismatic, public persona yet she had no personal support. She died sad and lonely.

MIRIAM NEFF

If her body of believers had held her accountable, as the prophet Nathan did King David, what might have happened? What can we learn from our sister's stumble as well as her climb to mountain peaks?

If we find ourselves in leadership, we should make sure we are never alone. Every human needs a friend within accountability range.

✒ **Find a friend who offers more than a handshake, who offers the grasp of accountability.**

I now realize how true it is that God does not show favoritism but accepts people from every nation who fear him and do what is right.

Acts 10:34–35 (NIV with my paraphrase)

*M*esses in women's lives are the stuff of great movements and great organizations to help people.

Mothers Against Drunk Drivers was founded by a mother whose child was killed by an inebriated human who made bad choices and created more than a mess.

Concerned Women of America was founded by Beverly LaHaye who saw families being harmed and even destroyed by the neglect and deafness of politicians and institutions within the beltway of our capital. She has marshaled a 625,000 voice "choir" to speak on behalf of families.

Clara Barton founded the American Red Cross because of the suffering and death she saw, smelled, heard, and touched. With the Civil War killing grounds as the womb of her passion, she birthed an organization that works to heal wherever war and suffering happen.

While the name Sister Helen Miller is not well known on earth, as Sister Mom she is beloved to the pregnant teens who come to Project Hope in Chicago. Since its inception eight years ago, she has acted on her conviction that "we've got to keep trying to educate people." She lives in a public housing apartment and clearly states her wish that her girls "could get out of here."† She is their assistant, their advocate on their path from dependence to independence.

God sees us as unrestricted by the tough stuff of life. He sees our potential as greater than any mess in our lives. He sees us with strength we do not know we have. He sees us with reserves of ideas and creativity. He sees us with the persistence to finish races even when we sometimes regret starting to run. He sees us exactly the way he made us.

✍ **The reverential fear of God is his only qualification for equal opportunity in his service. A mess may be the beginning for a positive movement.**

---

†Barbara Brotman, "Sister Mom," *Chicago Tribune*, 23 June 1993, 2.

MIRIAM NEFF

If anyone loves me, she will obey my teaching. My Father will love her, and we will come to her and make our home with her. She who does not love me will not obey my teaching.

John 14:23–24 (NIV with female pronouns)

*W*ho loves God? The woman who obeys him. And what woman might that be? Obedience is not easily measured. Others can create a quiz, but no one else can give us an obedience quotient, a test grade.

Our culture asks, "Does it work? Is it useful?" Our Father's criterion is different.

There were times in Jesus' life when observers questioned whether his obedience was useful. Throwing out the money changers in the temple did not mean they were not back the next week acting as if nothing had happened. Dying on display did not appear to be useful obedience at that moment. I imagine his women followers questioned

Jesus' obedience to God the night after he relinquished his life. After all, wasn't the Messiah supposed to accomplish something on earth?

Useful obedience is a hard call. It cannot be detected in a freeze-frame snapshot.

Useful obedience is something to think about, but the final call is God's. Useful obedience means matching what we do with God's goals. I'm often inclined to think that useful obedience means I must see results today, at the latest. I mean, give me an assignment where I can see, count, or hear that *something* happened. Martha will empathize with me when we get to heaven.

Well, God seems to be able to accomplish quite a bit through the unheard (by other people), unseen, untallied prayers of his saints. God has assigned some of his women and men to just pray. Actions unseen, results unseen, none are beyond God's providence.

✒ **God is the only One who can see far enough and with true world vision to decide what is useful. He calls it, we obey.**

Sisters, think of what you were when you were called. Not many of you were wise by human standards; not many were influential; not many were of noble birth. . . . Let her who boasts boast in the Lord.

1 Corinthians 1:26, 31 (NIV with female nouns)

"*S*end me your resume."

We prepare a list of everything impressive we can remember. We rename a lowly job to make it sound substantial. We dredge up old awards and certifications and ponder the right contacts and connections to write in the reference blanks.

I remember the selection process for a sorority. As I trouped from house to house, from one coffee to another tea, I dreaded the one question always asked: "And where are you from, Mimi?"

How do you describe a farm town, a town without even

one stop sign on the main highway going through it? How do you appear wealthy in Kresge's five-and-dime store flats?

When Jesus chose us, he had in mind a calling for us. He did not request a resume and then match our past to his assignments, or our achievements to a list on his job board. Oh, he can use all that stuff, but he may choose not to. In either case, whether what we do is infinitesimal or grandiose, those accomplishments are nothing compared to being the Lord's daughter.

✒ **Just call me the Lord's. I'm proud of it.**

I press on toward the goal to win the prize for which God has called me heavenward in Christ Jesus.

Philippians 3:14 (NIV)

$\mathcal{I}$ wonder if Paul thought of Mary, the mother of Jesus when he wrote to the Philippians about tenacity. I'm sure he heard many accounts of her life from eyewitnesses.

Mary, while pregnant with Jesus, went to visit her cousin Elizabeth. She needed another person to share her vision, her fears, and her joy. Elizabeth could almost understand. She, too, had experienced a miracle and probably had her own fears.

I'm sure, though, that when Jesus was killed, Mary's pain was like no other mother's pain in all of history. After all, there was no one else like her Son Jesus. She had no choice but to bear this awful pain alone. But in another sense, paradoxically, her mother grief was universal. Every mother whose child has been torn from her by tragedy suffers with Mary.

While God gave Mary an incredible and challenging assignment at a young age, he never abandoned her or left her without words from himself or comfort from others. What precious compassion for Jesus, even in his dying agony, to tell his friend John to care for Mary as his own mother. I imagine she heard those words in her ears for months and years to come, comforting her through memories and everyday struggles.

He always met her exactly where she was and gave her enough from his hand to enable her to make it through.

Tenacity.

From her words as a teen mother-to-be, to the hill where she watched her child leave her world, she showed us how to press on. "I am the Lord's servant. . . . May it be to me as you have said" (Luke 1:38 NIV).

✐ **Let us become a chorus of twenty-first century sisters saying, "We are the Lord's servants. May it be to us as you have said."**

MIRIAM NEFF

I press on to take hold of that for which Christ Jesus took hold of me. Philippians 3:12 (NIV)

How do we take hold of Jesus' calling for us?

For starters, think about your top five values.

What do you value most? Consciously choose an action you can take this week, no matter how insignificant it may seem, to affirm one of your important values.

Do you value work? Do you value your sisters? Maybe you could help a struggling sister fill out a job application. Every time we take positive action on our values, we become stronger within.

Do you value the earth God created? Collect some in a pot on your windowsill and grow dill or parsley. Bring some to a coworker. Insignificant? Not when you have affirmed one of your important values.

When our actions affirm our values, we grow. Imagine where the paths might lead for women who value work, for women who value their sisters, for women who value God's earth.

We grow because our actions strengthen our convictions. Our sisters are encouraged in a discouraging world. They see that values are more than talk. Onlookers get a message: Jesus is in us for a purpose.

No book or seminar or evangelical expert can choose for you. Think about your priorities. Then affirm your values before the Lord and take action.

✐ **Lord, I leave my Bible open today as my reminder and my pledge to you that my values will result in a new action today.**

They do not plead the case of the fatherless to win it, they do not defend the rights of the poor.

Jeremiah 5:28 (NIV)

Though my father and mother forsake me, the LORD will take me up (receive me).

Psalm 27:10 (NIV with my paraphrase)

Sometimes even the department with a clear mandate does not get the job done. Children go hungry and the poor are a platform for rhetoric, not people with cold, empty hands.

We have large organizations, bureaucracies with a worthwhile assignment, and processes that are supposed to provide for the needs of people who seem to have no advocate. Any person with charisma can get on the right float in a parade and wave whether they are dedicated to the cause or not. This is not a new problem; the Pharisees were

SISTERS OF THE HEART

the spiritual standard-bearers of their day. And they hardly raised the spiritual standard of Israel.

I am discouraged that our departments assigned to care for children cannot get the job done. Good intentions do not equal results.

But people who bumble and organizations without integrity are never the final word. The Mother Teresas of this world show us that God will use any person with compassion in her heart to defend his children. Help does not always come from where we expect it.

Mother Teresa embodies two living messages:

- Don't despair; your help may come from the unexpected. Don't give up; give God a chance to work.

- Don't devalue your potential. Mothers Against Drunk Drivers was started by an ordinary mother who cared. One widow who shared her last bottle of oil was able to feed her family for months.

You and I may be someone's defender or provider.

✐ **Lord, I see their need. What should I do?**

The angel of the LORD found Hagar near a spring in the desert . . . And he said, "Hagar, servant of Sarai, where have you come from, and where are you going?"   Genesis 16:7–8 (NIV)

She gave this name to the LORD who spoke to her: "You are the God who sees me," for she said, "I have now seen the One who sees me."

        Genesis 16:13 (NIV)

*H*agar is the first African woman who appears in Scripture. She was the Egyptian slave of Sarah, probably intelligent, strong, and attractive. She was selected by Sarah to be the birth mother of her child. When life got tough she thought God had a blind spot, and she was in it.

Some of my sisters feel they are invisible. While we all feel unseen at times, my black and Hispanic friends find this especially troubling. They feel unnoticed, unheard, and unimportant. Hagar had reason to feel the same way. Read her story in Genesis 16. God hears her cry. She is the first person mentioned in Scripture who is led to water by God and enabled to give it to another. Water, in Scripture, symbolizes spiritual life.

Hagar was transformed. She was willing to meet God in a new way, to adventure back to circumstances I personally would have avoided. No wonder she gave God a special name: "You are the God who sees me."

She teaches me a lesson.

✍ **In God's eyes there are no invisible women.**

*Praise be to the God and Father of our Lord Jesus
Christ, the Father of compassion and the God of all
comfort, who comforts us in all our troubles, so that
we can comfort those in any trouble with the comfort
we ourselves have received from God.*

2 Corinthians 1:3–4 (NIV)

*Women at ease have contempt for misfortune as the
fate of those whose feet are slipping.*

Job 12:5 (NIV with female noun)

*H*ave you ever poured out your personal tragedy to a friend whose life has been relatively trouble free? She looks at you blankly, may say she's sorry, but has no real comfort to offer.

But tell a friend who has also gone through deep waters, whose child has run away, who has been abandoned by someone she trusted, who has lost what she once treasured and felt she could not exist without. This friend offers comfort that reaches your pain, a soul hug that presses back the loneliness in your bones, words that soothe whether they give solutions or not.

To have slipping feet is not a contemptible characteristic. Hard times in life need be no secret. When I have closeted myself in my own personal tragedies, I postpone the benefits of being comforted by friends. I deny myself and others access to their powerful prayers.

What if our sister's story is one we'd rather not hear? Cold and judgmental treatment seldom helps a slipping sister. The God of all comfort is not surprised or shocked by tragedy. Neither should we be. Accept his comfort and then share it with a sister.

✍ **Trouble looks terminal, but it's the tunnel to compassion.**

There is neither Jew nor Greek, slave nor free, male nor female, for you are all one in Christ Jesus.

Galatians 3:28 (NIV)

*W*alls: barriers that send a message—you can't go from here to there. I stood peering over a wall that barred me from a special section of the Wailing Wall. I could not enter because I am a woman.

Invisible walls: lines on a city map that send a message. If you are the wrong color you cannot buy real estate here.

Invisible walls around a pulpit: If you are not a male, don't bring your gift here regularly. Don't preach.

There will be walls in heaven, jasper walls. While the streets will be paved with the purest of gold, and the wall foundations will be precious stones, the wall will be made of a stone not known for its value or brilliance: jasper, clear as crystal, see-through, opaque, transparent. And we'll all be inside.

There will be no temple walls in heaven because there will be no temple. God himself and Jesus are heaven's temple. We can walk together, talk together, worship together, live together.

No walls between people. No wonder they call it heaven.

✍ **Let's practice on earth the unity of heaven. If we can't remove the wall, at least we can be a door with a drawbridge and a welcome mat.**

*Blessed is the woman who does not walk in the
    counsel of the wicked or stand in the way of
    sinners or sit in the seat of mockers.
But her delight is in the law of the LORD, and on
    his law she meditates day and night.
She is like a tree planted by streams of water, which
    yields its fruit in season
and whose leaf does not wither.
Whatever she does prospers.*

Psalm 1:1–3 (NIV with female pronouns)

*Can a blind woman lead a blind woman? Won't
they both fall?*   Luke 6:39 (NIV with my paraphrase)

*I*t takes a rare, strong woman not to take on the behavior, then the ideas, and finally the values of those she's with. Sometimes we clone our companions. Old married folks even begin to look alike. "You are who you are with"—at times, anyway.

First we walk alongside another woman. We hear her talk; her counsel filters through our grid of beliefs and convictions.

Sounds good, doesn't it? We stop and stand soaking in what feels good of our new companion's company. But we are strong enough to be ourselves. We stand among them but are not of them.

The refrain of life's musical chairs begins. When the music stops we must sit down or be left out to stand out in the crowd. We grab for a chair and sit down. We are a stationary part—of the wrong crowd.

How did it happen?

A little at a time. Bit by bit. Thought by thought. Walking down the wrong road, standing soaking in the new surroundings, sitting down to get comfortable—all done to fit in.

Now, how do we get out? Usually our blurred vision makes it dangerous to just reach out for any hand. The person we walked in with is an unlikely candidate.

It is important for me to first remember my Creator. "God, you made me. I can't see my way out. Please tell me the first tiny step I can take." We begin by obeying simple instructions.

"Thank you, Lord; you know I'm here." We praise him.

🖋 Lord, I'll settle for a trickle of your water compared to a river of pollution. Weary and withered won't be a permanent condition. I choose to walk with you.

Judge nothing before the appointed time; wait till the Lord comes. He will bring to light what is hidden in darkness and will expose the motives of women's hearts. At that time each will receive her praise from God.   1 Corinthians 4:5 (NIV with female nouns)

5:30 A.M. Black sky littered with star diamonds. I stretch on my morning run looking into the heavens. The acrid, sweet smell of wet, turning leaves tells me that the black silhouettes of trees surrounding me will become raging red, yellow, and orange when the autumn sun strips the night of its blackness.

Somehow, as I look up into the heavens, the conflicts cluttering my mind, conflicts I must face later in the day, seem as infinitesimal and distant as the tiniest star winking above me.

Inner frustration over communications gone sour, contract dispute, stretched checkbook, and my own shrunken enthusiasm subsides. The God of the universe reminds me that he is the *only* one whose opinion matters. "Who are you trying to please? Who are you trying to impress, daughter of mine?"

From the expanse above me, the stars twinkle comfort and the blackness soothes like soft velvet. How small my day's trivia seem compared to the comfort of the Maker of the universe.

✒ **How big are our problems? How big is God? Not to worry.**

Now this is what the LORD Almighty says: "Give careful thought to your ways. You have planted much, but have harvested little. You eat, but never have enough. You drink, but never have your fill. You put on clothes, but are not warm. You earn wages, only to put them in a purse with holes in it."

Haggai 1:5 (NIV)

$\mathscr{T}$he harder I work, with any increase in income, the more offers come in my mail for more charge cards. "You, select resident [love the personal touch] . . . You, Ms. Mess [what mailing list keeps misspelling my name?], are entitled to an increase in your charging limit. We have conveniently enclosed blank checks so that you can indulge yourself at the mall."

Frankly, I do not need their help to overspend. I need no external prompting to imagine things I "need," to hunger for more. Yet my life is abundant by any measure.

Too much feels like too little, if God is not in it. The days of the month can outlast the dollars of any paycheck.

When Paul said he was content in any state, he had little (Phil. 4:12). Living in abundance, the challenge of contentment remains real. A full hand neither means a loose grasp nor contentment.

Left to God's multiplication tables, when we put our needs in his hands, he's a radical, generous provider, especially in the category of peace.

He who gave us the ability to plant, deserves to supervise the harvest.

*Men and women look at the outward appearance,
but the LORD looks at the heart.*

1 Samuel 16:7 (NIV with female noun)

*C*orporate image makers believe that women should spend 10 percent of their salary on clothing. It is interesting that this is identical to God's tithe in the Old Testament. I would profit by comparing my annual clothing expenditures to my kingdom tithes. Our Creator says to Miriam, "Where your treasure is, there your heart will be also" (Luke 12:34 NIV).

Fifty-three million women need something to wear to work. I recently surveyed twelve hundred Christian women. Sixty-one percent are employed full time and an additional 12 percent part time. Simply put, work is a factor in most Christian women's appearance.

Scripture turns statistics upside down. "Till your field and then build your house." In other words, "Work and

SISTERS OF THE HEART

earn an income, then decide, based on your priorities, what money will go for necessities and lifestyle stuff."

Working in a public school, a casual, inexpensive wardrobe is fine for me. I can be salt in my world on a lower budget than my friend who, as a lawyer, practices in two states—a warm one and a cold one. Our choices are different. Did you know that Disney has a dress code for interns and employees? There *is* a Disney look, and it's not mouse ears. The airlines specify more than the uniform. We make choices based on priorities and work, and appearance *is* important.

✍ **Lord, it is more important for you to groom my heart than all that I do about appearance.**

*Throw off everything that hinders and the sin that
so easily entangles, and let us run with perseverance
the race marked out for us.*   Hebrews 12:1 (NIV)

Sister, do you know the feeling of acting on the outside
in a way that does not reflect your inner values? We disaf-
firm the woman God created us to be when our actions
contradict our values. Action based on truth strengthens us.
Each time we act disloyally to ourselves, perhaps acting on
someone else's value, we defeat ourselves. We get tangled.
We can't run.

God always calls us to integrity with others and the
woman in the mirror.

Some of us must begin the race with small steps and
small statements. Being honest with God means we must
be honest with ourselves. We must look at our own behavior
and ask the tough questions. "Does this demonstrate what
I value? Or, am I tangling myself?"

And what if Jesus asks us to sell everything and follow him? Will we suggest other options to Jesus when he asks us to sell all? Might we walk away—and then turn back offering a compromise?

"Jesus, how about a 90 percent donation and 10 percent in a socially accountable mutual fund? And I would live off the mutual fund when I retire. Let's negotiate."

"Jesus, following you means staying on the road, literally, following on a dusty path. Remember my allergies? You've already got a crowd. Wouldn't one more just be a bother? Giving up the 'stuff' is no problem, but the 'following' part is."

"Wait a minute. Give to the poor? I heard that you told your disciples that all gifts did not need to go to the poor. Remember? I know you heal them and feed them sometimes. But from what I hear of your teachings, bringing the poor out of poverty is not your main goal. That's what I think too. My family has always worked hard, followed the rules, and it's paid off. I'd just have a hard time giving *everything* I've got to the poor. Maybe part of my wardrobe and some of my furniture, but not everything."

When Jesus asked the rich person to give away what he had, Jesus was laying the barometer face up. There was a choice to make, and no doubt, onlookers judged the man on his decision. Priority in his life was being revealed by the

MIRIAM NEFF

barometer of money. Jesus was giving him the opportunity to see what entangled him.

✍ **Truth untangles from the inside out. Only then can we run.**

Do not be anxious about anything, but in everything, by prayer and petition, with thanksgiving, present your requests to God. And the peace of God, which transcends all understanding, will guard your hearts and your minds in Christ Jesus.   Philippians 4:6-7 (NIV)

She's in control of her job . . . her kids . . . her marriage. So she doesn't have a worry in the world.

The company decides to downsize and she's unemployed; her teenage daughter runs away from home; her husband abandons her. What happens to the woman in control? She relinquishes what she could not own. She releases that which her tight grasp could not hold forever.

At precisely the point in life where we discover our world is out of control, God shows us he had a better plan in the first place. Out of control proves to be a safe life space when you give God jurisdiction over your career, family, and personal passions.

Fast tracking to a lifestyle that meets our wishes is possible. Women can do it with grit, persistence, and a few breaks along the way. Goals look promising and are achievable. But I must be careful of that fine line between my effort and accountability and my inclination to trust my control, crowding out God.

Even if I can gain for myself all that I want, I will be a poor woman. I will be anxious trying to make it all happen. What I can acquire are slim provisions compared to what God can provide.

✍ **God's plan is always best, and his peace is our bonus.**

And my God will meet all your needs according to his glorious riches in Christ Jesus.

Philippians 4:19 (NIV)

$\mathcal{M}$y two sisters suffered financially after their divorces. Both tell me that, while the divorce itself was the greatest blow to their sense of being a worthy person, their resulting poverty was one quick follow-up kick. The inclination to believe that their worth depended on either their marital status or their pocketbook simply demanded reconsideration in the devastation.

In time, they both came to believe and live by Paul's words: "I know what it is to be in need, and I know what it is to have plenty. I have learned the secret of being content in any and every situation, whether well fed or hungry, whether living in plenty or in want" (Phil. 4:12 NIV).

One sister, having moved from a nine-room home to a two-room apartment to a one-room boarder with kitchen

SISTERS OF THE HEART

privileges, struggled to rediscover who she was. Although money was certainly not her idol before, she found it hard to separate what she had and where she lived from who she was.

Recently we walked to the Hudson River. I studied her face as she watched the ducks bobbing in a cattail-rimmed cove. Satisfaction smoothed the crinkles on her face, crinkles carved by life through tough times. This woman's real needs have been met.

My other sister, on her own for three years now, offered me a cup of coffee in her new accommodations. She reached for the coffee pot that sat on top of the refrigerator—the only available spot for it in her new home. One-room studios in converted old "painted-lady" homes are not known for spacious cabinets or counter space.

I cleared a space on her couch—and bed—for our tray. Thank goodness for the familiar plants and ostrich feathers in the window. I knew she was still herself. Everything changed on the outside, but her love of color, living things, and unique objects remained.

Her bank account may measure her as poor. But her soul is not poor. I have never seen her more contented; she reminds me of her happy, five-year-old self.

Time and circumstance have certainly had their way with our sisters today. But God's promise has not changed.

His vow does not depend on a whimsical judge's heart or accumulated joint wealth. He is God. His vow can be trusted.

⤨ **God was God yesterday; God is God today; God will be God tomorrow. Good.**

Give thanks to the LORD, for he is good. . . .
Give thanks to the God of gods. . . .
Give thanks to the Lord of lords . . .
  to him who alone does great wonders . . .
  who by his understanding made the heavens . . .
  who spread out the earth upon the waters . . .
  who made the great lights . . .
  the sun to govern the day . . .
  the moon and stars to govern the night. . . .

To the One who remembered us in our low estate . . .
  and freed us from our enemies . . .
  and who gives food to every creature. . . .
Give thanks to the God of heaven.

Psalm 136:1–9, 23–26 (NIV)

Sometimes when life seems chaotic and light doesn't shine into the dismal space of our world, we fast. We fast

SISTERS OF THE HEART

as a discipline to remind our body that God is in control rather than our physical needs of the moment. We fast in desperation to refocus on God alone; there are no other answers.

These words from Psalm 136 are a good ending to a fast. I like to take a small meal, closet myself alone, read Scripture, and listen. My focus returns to God's strength and creativity. My focus returns to his provision for feeding his great whales and tiny insects. My dismal space seems brighter, chaos takes a diminished priority in his universe.

Fasting may not change the world, but surely it changes me. It reminds me that while *fast* means speedy or swift most of the time, it also means loyal, connected, tight. On dark days, that may be my only light.

✍ **Lord, thank you for good coffee and toast, a feast when in your presence.**

Keep on loving each other as sisters. Do not forget to entertain strangers, for by so doing some people have entertained angels without knowing it.

Hebrews 13:1–2 (NIV with female noun)

$\mathcal{A}$n inner circle of friends is more than comforting. It's necessary in our helter-skelter, disconnected world. But when there are no strangers in our circles, we're in danger of being too comfortable. Strangers bring new ideas, unmet needs, and fresh opportunities to test our thinking and to challenge our easy complacency. Strangers change hospitality from a good idea to a test of faith and obedience. Strangers bring the opportunity to offer a cup of cold water to God's emissaries in disguise.

I need to remember that when I see my son's friends at my kitchen table. Last week I pulled up a chair and we talked about their faith, how Joseph Smith who founded Mormonism is different from D. L. Moody, a turn-of-the-century Christian evangelist. As the dishes dried, we spoke of women and men, roles in society, and where we find truth.

Who is a stranger? A girlfriend's out-of-town relative at our holiday gathering. A preteen at our child's birthday party, with braces and wild hair. Our young adult son's woman friend of the month. We don't know which is the angel unaware. And that is precisely God's point. We entertain without knowledge that there will be a return. That's being a sister.

 Angels enter an open door and an open heart.

The king was shaken. He went up to the room over the gateway and wept. As he went, he said: "O my son Absalom! My son, my son Absalom! If only I had died instead of you—O Absalom, my son, my son!"   2 Samuel 18:33 (NIV)

*W*hy does a parent weep for a rebellious child? Absalom planned to kill his father, combining a corporate, as well as political, raid. David's inner circle expected him to be pleased at the news of Absalom's death. A son of rebellion, exiled for murder, was now dead. Why not forget Absalom existed?

Some mothers today share David's anguish. Some of us understand a love that cannot forget, a love that cannot give up, a love that simply will not die.

In spite of murder, distant whereabouts unknown, still that glimmer of hope-shaped love persists. My precious prodigal may turn around. His heart of stone may someday be ground fine as powder and be pliable. Twisted thinking may become straight.

Never underestimate the love, the connection, the steel bond between a parent and her child.

To every mother who understands: Never apologize for that feeling, though onlookers may think you a fool.

I would rather love my child too long than give up too soon. I would rather die with that hope-shaped glimmer in my heart than die without faith. I would rather live trusting the Lover of all prodigals who loves my beloved child with a greater love than a mother's love.

✐ **Love never gives up.**

MIRIAM NEFF

Sisters, don't be like children. Be infant-like when it comes to evil. But be 100 percent adult women when it comes to understanding.

1 Corinthians 14:20 (NIV with my paraphrase)

"I'll think about that tomorrow." We know the story and the heroine who made that line famous. The appeal of childhood calls us back to years of innocence and abandon when the checkbook was someone else's problem, the charge card bill did not have our names on it, and there were no kids with our last names and genes. There are days I'd love to "think about that tomorrow." Give me a sandy beach where I can bury my head, a shopping mall where I can forget the mess at home.

But we are 100 percent adult now, and our Creator tells us we cannot be childlike when it comes to understanding. We're not in the Garden of Eden. Our world is not lush and green, but rather like salt flats around a dried pool. The age of innocence has passed. We are called to a new way of thinking. To be adult is to be accountable, to see the facts of our real world. We must pay for the purchase. Our children must be fed, clothed, reasoned with, raised.

We see the evil of the world around us, but we are like infants trusting that the powerful arms of our Creator will hold us when we cannot protect ourselves or fix what is wrong.

One hundred percent adult women. We are sisters who encourage each other to face today; sisters who make choices we can live with today even if tomorrow never comes; sisters who make choices we can live with tomorrow as accountable adults.

✐ **Today is tomorrow's foundation.**

*Then Salome and her sons, James and John, came
to Jesus, kneeling down asking something from
Him. And He said to her, "What do you wish?"
She said to Him, "Grant that these two sons of
mine may sit, one on your right hand and the other
on the left, in your kingdom."*

Matthew 20:20–21 (NKJV with my paraphrase)

*S*alome was making "mother noises." Maybe she thought Jesus owed her. After all, her sons left the family business; her husband had to keep fishing without their hands, without their energy, without their youth and vigor. The family's assets must have been affected.

Or maybe she thought it was an expedient, forward-looking move to ensure her sons a political future. She had to know that Jesus was especially fond of John. Her vision of Jesus' kingdom, no doubt, was a near-future, political entity with potential.

And mothers can sometimes secure favors that grown men cannot. Which mother among us has not attempted some fancy footwork for the good of her children?

It did not work.

I wonder if Salome watched Jesus on the cross from a distance and had a fleeting vision of James on the cross to the left of him and John on the cross to the right?

Did her heart throb with agony for him and gratitude for the once unwelcome "No"?

And what is the lesson for women today?

We ask with our human eyes focused on the near-future, with a desire for position as we see the political lay of the land. We ask for our children and we ask for ourselves. Like Salome, we think we have the angles figured.

Let us drop to our knees both with body and soul and tell Jesus, "I am willing for you to choose my position. And given that it's your choice, Jesus, I am able to fill it.

"I'm willing for you to choose for my children. It's only wise. I'm limited with short-sightedness and a hunger for political plums. Grant that these children of mine may sit exactly where you assign them."

✍ **Bended knees and a willing heart produce the right request.**

*"Bring me a denarius and let me look at it."
They brought the coin, and he asked them, "Whose
portrait is this? And whose inscription?"*

"Caesar's," they replied.

*Then Jesus said to them, "Give to Caesar what
is Caesar's and to God what is God's."*

Mark 12:15–17 (NIV)

*Then God said, "Let us make woman and man in
our image, in our likeness."*

Genesis 1:26 (NIV with female noun)

*For we are God's masterpiece, created in Christ
Jesus to do good works, which God prepared in
advance for us to do.*

Ephesians 2:10 (NIV with my paraphrase)

*Before I was born the LORD called me; from my
birth he has made mention of my name.*

Isaiah 49:1 (NIV)

$\mathcal{I}$have God's imprint on me.

I am nobody's property but his. And he does not call me *property;* he calls me *masterpiece.*

Bearing God's imprint, I face today.

Bearing God's imprint, I face other people.

Bearing God's imprint, I face my coworkers, my relatives, my children, my parents, my mate.

Who is this woman looking back at me from the mirror? Behind my less-than-smooth complexion, crinkled eyes, and short nose, there is an image God wants to reflect of himself.

Remember, sister, you bear his imprint; you are his masterpiece.

$\mathcal{D}$ **There's a masterpiece in the mirror.**

*Therefore, sisters, since we have confidence to enter
the Most Holy Place by the blood of Jesus, by a new
and living way opened for us through the curtain,
that is, his body, and since we have a great priest
over the house of God, let us draw near to God
with a sincere heart in full assurance of faith,
having our hearts sprinkled to cleanse us from a
guilty conscience and having our bodies washed
with pure water.*

Hebrews 10:19–22 (NIV with female noun)

*W*e've been given a gold medal of God's approval.

Some days we turn it in to have it bronzed.

On those days we don't walk tall as though we trust.

We slouch like we're clobbered. We stoop like we're scared.

Our faces look tense like we're tainted.

But we're clean because we walked through the curtain.

We're gold because he said so.

 It is the Creator's right to label his product.

*If the ax is dull and its edge unsharpened, more
strength is needed but skill will bring success.*

Ecclesiastes 10:10 (NIV)

What you and I do not have is okay.

Grandma Hatie wrote with a stubby short pencil. But her words inspired her grandchildren, including me.

Abraham Lincoln read by candlelight. The things he learned reading God's opinion of a human soul changed the course of our nation.

Using our fingers to crumble clods of soil can begin a garden as well as digging with a hoe. Tools do not dictate what we produce. This little truth grows big when you use what you have in life.

Clara Barton was a nurse, not a surgeon. Healing and comfort occur all over the world today through the Red Cross because she used the skill she had.

Mother Teresa is neither theologian nor philosopher,

but she has made a compelling statement to the entire world about the value of any person. She has influenced politicians, presidents, and kings.

I accomplish little musing over degrees I don't have or resources beyond my reach. Credentials we lack and tools we don't have cannot prevent us from using what is in our hands. Dreaming may be a beginning. But action is the operative noun before success.

✍ **When I don't have what it takes, God looks even better.**

See, the Sovereign LORD comes with power, and his
arm rules for him.
See, his reward is with him, and his recompense
accompanies him.
He tends his flock like a shepherd: He gathers the
lambs in his arms
  and carries them close to his heart; he gently
  leads those that have young.

Isaiah 40:10–11 (NIV)

𝓗e is tender with you, dear mother. He sees your vulnerability. He cares when added responsibility exposes you to anxiety. He knows you become fatigued. He is not a do-it-all taskmaster. Rather, he is your gentle leader.

When Mary, the mother of Jesus, was given the promise that she would bear the Messiah, she did not receive a set of daily instructions. She continued to live a day at a time doing all the routine things of living. I assume that labor and delivery of her new son were as painful as most births.

New life usually means more work.

But new mothers need not dread the future.

The Giver of the gift will carry your child close to his heart. And he promises to lead you with his hand. He says so.

✍ **Fatigue and fear are signals to follow close.**

Therefore, my sisters, you whom I love and long for, my joy and crown, that is how you should stand firm in the Lord, dear friends!

Philippians 4:1 (NIV with female noun)

Slipping or slumping today? What action can you take to remind yourself that you are loved, longed for, a crown?

Are you mumbling, "But I'm supposed to practice self-denial and self-sacrifice." May I draw your attention to the *self* word? We must have a sense of self *created by God*, loved, and longed for before we can stand firm or give anything—including the love of God—away.

Ask yourself, "What kind of person am I at my best?" Not who do others want me to be, but rather, what inner qualities are God-created within? What talent or virtue is within? What action can I take to affirm this quality?

Remember *Chariots of Fire?* In one scene, the runner says to his sister, "God made me fast. And when I run, I feel his

131

pleasure." Then he *ran!* I imagine as he ran, the angels looked down and saw a crown on his head—invisible to human eyes, of course. And God was smiling.

I run with a smile on my face. I may be aging and slow, but, praise God, I'm still running. I don't run marathons or win prizes, but I run in our neighborhood and meet neighbors, dogs, and children. I think God delights in my running.

Sister, you can face each day knowing you are loved and longed for. Are you wired up for activity? Affirm that quality.

🖋 **Take action. God is smiling.**

You will know the truth, and the truth will set you free.   John 8:32 (NIV)

 $\mathcal{T}$ he most powerful lie that the evil one promotes in our minds is that Scripture is not our guide for life, that we must just bumble along the journey with no real answers to our questions, no hope for our dreams. The evil one's crooked tale goes like this: "This life is a test. It is only a test. If it had been an actual life, you would have received further instructions on where to go and what to do."

Women who believe the evil one's lies are slaves to fear and have no truth to stand on when their world quakes. They are slaves to ignorance when no one but God has answers, slaves by choice. I know how it feels to want to give up on a life of obedience. I know how it feels to have a sister tell me, "You can't give up. I won't let you give up."

These are days when we must take the hand of our sister who has sat down in the mud of a failed marriage and say, "I will coach you through. We'll talk together. I'll interpret for you in the midst of this confusion. You may not stay here in the mire."

These are days when sister must stand beside sister in the marketplace and say to whomever will listen, "You say you value families, then why this unfriendly policy toward mothers?"

Let us choose truth and declare it together. Freedom will follow.

✍ **Truth belongs everywhere: in the marketplace, the government, the family, and between sisters.**

The prayer of a righteous woman is powerful and effective.

James 5:16 (NIV with female pronoun)

"My prayer won't be heard, let alone answered," a sister sighs. "I'm hardly a righteous woman."

God whispers back, "But now a righteousness from me, apart from law, has been modeled to the world, to which the Law and the Prophets testify. This righteousness from me comes through faith in Jesus Christ to all who believe" (Rom. 3:21–22 NIV with my paraphrase). "Sister, it's my Son, not your worthiness that makes you righteous."

Have you heard it said that the ground is level at the foot of the cross? In other words, we are all in equal need of God's forgiveness. Except for the grace of Jesus, none of us could talk to God.

But there's more. The ground is level when we kneel to

pray. We are heard because we're wrapped in the wonderful royal, yet cozy, robe of Jesus' righteousness.

Sisters, let's pray.

🖋 **Every sister's voice has equal access to our Father.**

For he chose us in him before the creation of the world to be holy and blameless in his sight.

Ephesians 1:4 (NIV)

Your eyes saw my unformed body.
All the days ordained for me were written in your book before one of them came to be.

Psalm 139:16 (NIV)

One planned human being, wanted by my Father, chosen with good intentions. That's you; that's me.

What difference does it make in your life to know that God made a choice about you?

Most days that question never registers as I go through my day doing whatever task is before me. Recently I realized that my knowing that God made a choice for me *has* made a difference in my work.

A high school girl is pregnant. We talk. She chooses.

SISTERS OF THE HEART

A child is born.

Today a three-month-old charmer smiles at me from the photo gallery above my desk. The note on the back reads: "This little guy might not be here if it were not for you."

His mom is busy with classes, homework, feedings, baths, and diapering. School is interrupted by pediatrician visits. Sleep is interrupted by her infant's fussing. Social life no longer exists. Yet, this mother and student is more contented than many teens I know. She is mothering quite well.

Why choose life? Because he chose, we can choose. My *knowing* that he chose life for me mattered on that ordinary work day when a distraught young girl slipped into my office. And that makes all the difference.

🖊 **Choice is not an isolated event.**

All people are like grass,
    and all their glory is like the flowers of the field.
The grass withers and the flowers fall,
    because the breath of the LORD blows on them.
Surely the people are grass.
The grass withers and the flowers fall,
But the word of our God stands forever.

Isaiah 40:6–8 (NIV with my paraphrase)

*W*hat difference does my effort make? Do you ever feel like I do? Like wilted grass. Progress produces a blossom and then it begins to wilt? I understand discouragement at work. I want to be salt in the public school where I work. Yet I see the misinterpretation of the separation of church and state destroying public education. You work in a different place and probably see the Word of God squelched for different reasons.

Take courage. Here's what I saw yesterday.

SISTERS OF THE HEART

A cross woven of twigs was planted just off the school property at the street corner. Tragically, one year ago a student was killed there; the car in which he rode was hit by a semi. The students still remember. And they remembered him by reading from an open Bible. They prayed; they planted a cross.

Kids still bear the imprint of their Maker. The spiritual spark still exists. I saw it. Just off the school property.

✐ **Just when we feel like wilting, we are reminded, the Word of our Lord will always stand.**

*With this in mind, we constantly pray for you, that
our God may count you worthy of his calling, and
that by his power he may fulfill every good purpose
of yours and every act prompted by your faith.*

2 Thessalonians 1:11 (NIV)

*C*hristian women are satisfied with their work. Why?
We know that most tasks we do will have to be done again.
We know that in a short time, maybe a few years or even
months, there will be little lasting evidence that we accom-
plished what we're busy accomplishing.

Much of what we do is mundane, repetitious, very, very
ordinary indeed. Women are traditionally the secretaries of
the world, the sales clerks, receptionists, the caretakers of
living spaces, the ever-so-daily caregivers.

We sense in our hearts that our work is more than the
task at hand. Remember my research of Christian women
showed that the number one satisfaction, the reward that

ranked above a paycheck for employed Christian women, was the satisfaction they feel knowing their work is fulfilling their calling from God.

We value connecting people, adding beauty to the moment though it is temporary. We value adding that touch of quality to someone's life unconnected to dollars. We look back on a day of work with satisfaction for the unmeasurable, the unseen.

✍ **Our work is our mission. And God approves.**

Therefore, in the present case I advise you: Leave
these men alone! Let them go! For if their purpose
or activity is of human origin, it will fail. But if it
is from God, you will not be able to stop these men;
you will only find yourselves fighting against God.

Acts 5:38–39 (NIV)

$\mathscr{T}$he gutsy apostles inspired a Pharisee named Gama-
liel to say these words. Peter and company knew what they
were called to do and to say, and they would not give
up or shut up. These are good words for Christian sisters
struggling against the tide. I think of women who sense
God's calling to preach or teach. I think of women who
work driven by a passion for low-profile causes. They face
the normal obstacles of work—and a few more.

Criticism and obstacles can slow them down, soften
their voices, postpone the achievement of their goals. Deny-
ing them resources can divert them temporarily while they

discover God's provision elsewhere. Withholding affirmations can intensify their dependence on God.

But in the big picture—in other words, eternity—you lose, and they win.

To oppose sisters who hear God calling is a futile use of energy. If their call is from God, no one will be able to stop these women. Let's expend every ounce of our energy to advance God's purpose. Such action is much, much needed in this truth- and love-starved world.

✍ **Let's affirm the crusaders among us.**

For God so loved the world that he gave his one and only Son, that whoever believes in him shall not perish but have eternal life.   John 3:16 (NIV)

$\mathcal{S}$cripture tells me that God so loved you and me that he did not send a committee to save us. Thank God for that. He knows there's no way that one complex woman with her unique mind, emotions, body, and soul could find him on her own. He sends his Son to each of us individually to be our bridge. No board of directors dictates the way to God. The connection is always one to one.

In our everything-is-relative culture, when laws have confusing nuances and our workplace is a maze of policies, at least one truth is crystal clear.

Jesus is the one bridge to our Father who created us in love and wants to connect with us.

Our Father does not want a temporary relationship; he does not offer us conditional commitment. He offers us an environment for life not death, living not existing. The choice is clearly ours.

When we step onto the bridge of Jesus, we instantly become God's daughters. We have new positions, new living standards, new identities. We have the only life worth having.

🖋 **Sisters, let's spread the good word about our Bridge.**

Father, hallowed be your name, your kingdom come.
Give us each day our daily bread.
Forgive us our sins, for we also forgive everyone who
     sins against us.
And lead us not into temptation.   Luke 11:2-4 (NIV)

$\mathcal{P}$rayer is two-way communication. Like babies learning to talk, teens learning to express themselves, adults becoming articulate, praying is a process. Are parents any less attentive to their three-month-old daughter's babbling than they are to her sentences when she's five? Of course not.

Look at your home movies. You've probably filmed your child saying sweet nothings—and you think it's precious!

God listens to us because we are his daughters. Our infant understanding does not deafen his ears nor does our sophisticated philosophizing make them more sensitive.

When we cannot pray, cannot discover adequate words, saying to Jesus the prayer he taught his friends is an excellent beginning. Using his prayer as a model, write your own prayer in a notebook. When I am distracted, which is frequently, I write my prayers or talk to Jesus out loud.

No prayer is too long or too short for God to listen, consider, and answer. No babble is unintelligible, since he reads hearts. Length is not important to God. I write long prayers especially when crisis has turned into long-term burdens that I must carry. I don't believe God listens more closely to my long prayers than he has to others I've cried such as:

Help!
Ouch!
Is it ease-up time yet?
Thank you!

✐ **Just pray.**

*Give me neither poverty nor riches, but give me only
    my daily bread.
Otherwise, I may have too much and disown you
    and say, "Who is the LORD?"
Or I may become poor and steal, and so dishonor
    the name of my God.*   Proverbs 30:8–9 (NIV)

$\mathcal{O}$ur Creator tells us quite clearly that money is no measure for the women and men he created.

The temptation of the wealthy woman is to see her possessions as gains due to her superior intelligence, wit, beauty, or strength. (God's lucky to have me.)

The temptation of the poor woman is to believe she is somehow inferior. (God doesn't care so I'll take matters into my own hands.)

When I am tempted to judge other women using a dollar yardstick, I need to replace that urge with the facts about money from Scripture.

Money is temporary. It's an earthly thing with no eternal value of its own. Here today, gone tomorrow. Actually, in my household this summer with all four children driving, it's here this minute, gone the next. I used to say when my children were small that money was like butter hitting a hot griddle, gone in a sizzle. Today it seems that a hand grabs the butter ball before it hits the griddle. Money is temporary.

While we do not know other women's circumstances or the reasons for how they dress, where they live, or what they do with their dollars, we can accept that those facts are between them and their Creator. God knows what's behind the door, under the makeup, inside the skin.

𝒫 **Lord, I ask for daily bread only.**

*Show me, O LORD, my life's end and the number
of my days; let me know how fleeting is
my life.
You have made my days a mere handbreadth; the
span of my years is as nothing before you.*

Psalm 39:4-5 (NIV)

$\mathcal{I}$ am prone to ignore the treasures of the moment while thinking of what the future might bring. For many of us, there is an ever present dream bubble over our heads:

Three more months to promotion, then real life begins.

Two more years on this job, then I move on to real living.

They'll all be in school in eighteen months; I can't wait.

Retirement. If I can just hold on till then.

The final court date. Resolution. Life will begin.

The last one out of high school. Then I won't worry about answering the phone.

I remember this dream bubble from my childhood: If I could just be ten years old, have a double-digit age, I'd be a grown-up.

Other dream bubbles followed: If I could just get my college degree and get a real job, life would be a picnic forever.

When my last baby enters school, I will rest, drink a cup of coffee while it's still hot, take a nap in the afternoon if the previous day's work has gobbled up half the night's sleep.

Reaching a goal seldom shifted my focus to the moment I was living though I dreamed that it would. How does God teach us to treasure today? A surprise, almost losing something or someone we treasure, or a crisis can bring our focus back to the moment. We treasure today.

✍ **Keep me temporary, Lord. As my recovering sisters say, "One day at a time."**

Listen then to what the parable of the sower means: When anyone hears the message about the kingdom and does not understand it, the evil one comes and snatches away what was sown in her heart. This is the seed sown along the path. The one who received the seed that fell on rocky places is the woman who hears the word and at once receives it with joy. But since she has no root, she lasts only a short time. When trouble or persecution comes because of the word, she quickly falls away. The one who received the seed that fell among the thorns is the woman who hears the word, but the worries of this life and the deceitfulness of wealth choke it, making it unfruitful. But the one who received the seed that fell on good soil is the woman who hears the word and understands it. She produces a crop, yielding a hundred, sixty or thirty times what was sown.

Matthew 13:18–23 (NIV with female nouns)

SISTERS OF THE HEART

$\mathcal{T}$he first woman described in the above scripture just doesn't get it. She doesn't comprehend the idea of a God-shaped life. The concept disappears like a vapor.

The second woman gets the idea and is willing to accept a free ride, easy believism, a God-shaped life with no pressure points, no sacrifice, no switchbacks—only a smooth ride. Of course, free rides are short. Life guarantees trouble sooner or later. This woman abandons the adventure.

The third woman hears the message of her Maker and embraces his invitation to live a God-shaped life. When real life happens, she worries about the bad things in this imperfect world. Then she is deceived. "If God is powerful enough to make this world, why do bad things happen?" She doubts her Maker's word and lives stifled by her doubts and fears.

The last woman is our model. She hears the message of her Maker. She knows the world is scarred by the enemy and by people's choices against her Maker's wishes. She recognizes the tough stuff of life caused by humans acting like humans and knows her Maker did not wish it so. She simply believes and trusts his love for her. Her life is productive.

The thief of worry cannot touch what she has.

$\mathcal{D}$ **Understanding God is the secret to a worry-proof world.**

*Is not wisdom found among the aged? Does not long
life bring understanding?*   Job 12:12 (NIV)

*I*f you have teens or children of any age, there are
probably times you look at choices they make with hands
over your face, peeking out through slits between your
fingers.

And we *try* to talk to them.

Their ways are not our ways. We cannot fathom grow-
ing up with the information, entertainment, all the stuff
they have in their lives. Rather than concluding we have no
wisdom to offer them, remember Job's words.

Just surviving more years on the planet brings some
understanding, though not all we wish. Teens may figure
out a VCR more quickly than we. They may be able to
keep that irritating 12:00 from flashing twenty-four hours a
day. And, yes, they can microwave a decent meal. But shar-
ing our understanding can expose them to information they

could never glean simply because they have not been around as long as we have.

Our toddlers eventually outrun us. Our teens may finally outsmart us. However, they cannot pass us in accumulated years of experience. Instant wisdom is an oxymoron. They need all the wisdom they can get, theirs plus ours. It's that kind of world.

✐ **Let us never relinquish the goal of communication between generations.**

*In her heart a woman plans her course, but the
LORD determines her steps.*

Proverbs 16:9 (NIV with female noun)

$\mathcal{I}$ sat, many years ago, at my counselor position wishing to be an account executive. No matter that I was new to the profession and the company. Have you ever wished to be a mature blossom at the peak of beauty when in fact you were a bud? Or are you not yet a bud but rather an ordinary bulb in the ground that shows no resemblance to the future blossom?

God's invention of seasons offers wisdom that can be applied to us in our work. Training does not instantly translate to experienced judgment whether on our job, where we volunteer, or as parents. God knows this. Looking back on those months when I wished to be an account executive, I see God's wisdom in keeping me right where I was.

He knew me. He knew I needed to learn more about

real estate. He knew I needed to learn more about negotiating and team building. And he also knew the time and stress of that position as well as the needs of my four children.

He knows circumstances in our future and just what we need for those future appointments. It's fine to plan and prepare, and then commit the plan to God.

✐ **For his glory, a bulb becomes a bud, becomes a blossom. It's true of people too.**

*You have let go of the commands of God and are
holding on to the traditions of women.*

Mark 7:8 (NIV with female noun)

*G*et a job . . . stay at home . . . find the best caretaker . . .
take care of your *own* kids . . . use your God-given gifts . . .
you're a mom, other jobs must wait.

As in the Civil War, both sides claim God's blessing and
to be his truth bearers.

Even today, when the conflicts are no longer new or
fresh, it's the hottest topic at our lunch table at work. Young
women, middle-agers like me, and grandmothers at the table
each have strong feelings. And few agree.

As Christian women, we know the call of tradition is
not the same as the voice of God. As Christian women, we
know that choosing a new path with more opportunities is
not necessarily the same as God's path.

We are hasty to advise each other based on our own

SISTERS OF THE HEART

experiences and our opinions of God's opinion. Would it not be wiser if we advised each other, "Take your questions to your Maker"?

"Pray for direction. The choice is more important to him than you could ever imagine."

"How did God wire you up? What about the others you care about? What is doable? Can God bless the choice?"

"Sister, here's Scripture. Let's talk and pray."

When we hold on to him, the rest will fall into place.

✐ **God always blesses obedience.**

About the Author

Miriam Neff is a woman who wears many hats: She is a counselor in a public high school, mother of four, writer, and speaker. She is also the cohost (with Babbie Mason) of the radio show "A Sister's Heart" and is a contributing editor for *Christian Parenting Today*.

Miriam's previous books include *Women and Their Emotions, Helping Teens in Crisis, Working Moms: Survival to Satisfaction,* and *Devotions for Women in the Workplace*.

She lives in Kildeer, Illinois, with her husband and four children. Her hobbies include water skiing, reading, and traveling. She says she runs for sanity as well as health and hopes she's hanging on to both.